President Trump's Coronavirus Disaster

AN OPEN LETTER TO THE NATION

ISBN: 9798672733876

FORWARD

Surely, we all can see: Our nation is based on trust and we must deal in the truth.

.

CONTENTS

ACKNOWLEDGMENTS
Much of the event and general information in this extensive letter is from the news media, especially The Washington Post, The New York Times, The COVID Tracking Project, CNN and MSNBC.

1 INTRODUCTION

When Franklin D. Roosevelt (FDR) came into office in 1932, the United States was well into the Great Depression, the worst financial disaster in the nation's history. The country was also in a leadership crisis with President Herbert Hoover, who was not prepared to deal with the financial demise and let things get worse by not taking any meaningful actions to reverse the course of the situation. In his inaugural address, FDR saw clear actions that needed to be taken to get the country out of the economic downfall and pointed the way forward as a nation with the rallying assertion, **"The only thing we have to fear is fear itself."**

The United States is again in a crisis, the novel coronavirus disease 2019 (COVID-19) pandemic. Again, the nation is in a presidential leadership crisis. Similar to Hoover, President Trump was totally unprepared and does not have the leadership skills to deal with a serious national crisis and made things worse, much worse. This comprehensive letter clearly demonstrates that President Trump made the coronavirus COVID-19 into a national disaster. The way forward suggests updating the above assertion to: **"The only thing we have to fear is fear of Trump himself."**

President Trump's Coronavirus Disaster

This mini-book discusses President Trump's coronavirus leadership failures and how they affected the nation throughout the crisis from January into August 2020. The impact of President Trump's leadership failures and his apparent disregard for the well being of the American people cannot be overstated. For example, President Trump's leadership failures include: (a) inept decision in 2018 to dismantle the Pandemic Directorate in the White House left the government without a sentinel group to look out for, plan and direct the government to deal with a pandemic crisis, (b) ignoring early formal U.S. intelligence community warnings on 3 January 2020 and later and early Centers for Disease Control and Prevention (CDC) take-action warnings, (c) denial of the coronavirus pandemic for over 2 months, which delayed meaningful actions by the government and enabled the virus to spread, (d) deceiving the public with stunningly inept and thoughtless statements, such as "the virus is a hoax" and on 26 February "the number of cases will go from 15 to close to zero in a few days". These demonstrated leadership failures left the country totally unprepared to deal with the crisis and with no action plan in place.

After the virus was spreading in the U.S. for over two months (and after the stock markets dropped drastically), President Trump declared a National Health Emergency on 13 March. This action was too little and too late. In New York City, the hospitals did not have nearly enough medical equipment, beds, staff or testing capability to deal with the crisis. It was indeed a catastrophe; patients were dying and the dead were taken out of the hospitals and stored in refrigerated tractor trailer trucks. Because of the lack of medical personal protective equipment nurses and doctors were getting sick, with some dying. By the end of April, the coronavirus "EXPLODED" to over 1 million confirmed cases and 65,837 deaths in the U.S. These numbers are staggering and represent a health disaster! The U.S. had about one-third of the total global confirmed cases and about one-quarter of the number of global deaths. The number of jobless benefit claims reached roughly 30 million in six weeks, with 20.5 million jobs lost in April alone. These numbers are also staggering and represent a financial disaster!

After states shut down their economies and closed schools, the number of coronavirus cases per day in the country slowly decreased through May. President Trump was urging economies to open (since before Easter) and the CDC provided guidelines for doing this. However, many state governors and citizens, seeing President Trump downplay the dangers of the coronavirus, ignored the guidelines. As a result, the coronavirus experienced a second surge in many of the cluster areas across the county. These multiple surges, when added together, were producing over 65,000 confirmed cases per day and reached a total of over 4 million confirmed cases by 23 July 2020 and over 5 million by 8 August. The virus had "EXPLODED" a second time in June and July, with over 1 million confirmed cases in each of the last two 16-day segments.

President Trump's leadership failures are rooted in his innate leadership flaws. A list of President Trump's innate leadership flaws is provided in the next section. During the coronavirus crisis, his leadership flaws were seen as being connected to his leadership failures. In the third section, demonstrations of President Trump's leadership failures are presented and connected to both Trump's leadership flaws and the chronological events of the crisis. The fourth section explains the "EXPLOSIVE" exponential growth of cases and deaths that occurred during peak periods of the virus and, using models, shows how the total number-of-deaths are linked to Trump's delays in social distancing implementation and downplaying of the coronavirus dangers. The fifth section presents a coronavirus event summary and the last section presents the conclusion and final thoughts, which includes a discussion on the President's innate leadership attributes _and_ flaws and how they combined to help explain the success and failure of the president during his career.

2 PRESIDENT TRUMP'S LEADERSHIP FLAWS

President Trump has demonstrated apparent innate leadership flaws throughout his presidency. The flaws became more apparent during the Mueller investigation and his Impeachment process. During the coronavirus crisis, his leadership flaws became even more apparent as the president took part in the daily Coronavirus Task Force Meetings. President Trump was making statements that were quickly proved to be wrong, even ridiculous. Further, President Trump's leadership flaws became linked to his leadership failures, which impacted the public, as more people became sick and died or lost their jobs. Trump's innate Leadership Flaws, most apparant with the coronavirus crisis, are listed; his:

(1) Refusal to deal in the truth; (President Trump was not honest with himself or the American public.)

(2) Inept, thoughtless actions; (Sometimes these actions are ego-driven and self-promotional.)

(3) Thoughtless Inactions; (The resulting delays in acting against coronavirus pandemic were a major factor in the number

of deaths recorded.)

(4) Lack of understanding, over-confidently ignoring information from experts; (The experts include the U.S. intelligence community, the CDC and his cabinet.);

(5) Lack of general knowledge;

(6) Demeaning and blaming others without merit (including the truthful news media, the CDC and the U.S. intelligence community);

(7) Lack of concern and respect for others;

(8) Inability to plan and organize future actions; (In the President's words: "I don't worry about anything. I just do what needs to be done.")

(9) Inability to select top quality staff;

(10) Inability to work with others, intellectually, socially, ethically and legally; (The White House has seen an extraordinary turnover in the Trump Presidency.)

(11) Inability to know right from wrong and Lack of Ethical Standards;

(12) Inability to envision future consequences of his actions;

(13) Inept, incorrect statements, false and misleading statements; (Many of President Trump's misleading statements are said with an ego-driven, self-promotional or bragging motivation.)

President Trump's Coronavirus Disaster

Upon reviewing the list of President Trump's innate Leadership Flaws, it can be seen that many of his Leadership Flaws can be viewed as Character Flaws, or his general Lack of Ethical Standards. The Character Flaws are treated as Leadership Flaws if they contribute to his inability to lead the nation, as President of the United States.

3 PRESIDENT TRUMP'S CORONAVIRUS LEADERSHIP FAILURES

The following discussion presents events in chronological order which demonstrate the leadership failures of President Trump and his administration in dealing with the coronavirus pandemic. **Trump's failings amplified the coronavirus pandemic crisis into the nation's worst crisis since World War II.** These leadership failures are numbered, the corresponding innate leadership flaw is provided, and the specific leadership failure is dated, explained and discussed in the following:

(A) EARLY TRUMP FAILURES

(1) [**Inept Action and Inability to Envision the Future Consequences of the Action.**] In 2018, President Trump dismantled the National Security Council Directorate for Global Health Security and Biodefense at the White House. The Directorate was established after the successful minimization of the Ebola crisis in 2014. The Directorate goal was to prepare for the next disease outbreak and prevent it from becoming an epidemic or pandemic. While the Trump administration says the Directorate was re-organized, the previous administration's

director Dr. Beth Cameron says, **"Trump closed it."** **History may view this Trump administration blunder as one of the worst mistakes ever by a president of the United States.**

(2) [**Inability to Select Top-Level Staff, Inability to Work with Others**] During President Trump's selection of his cabinet and staff, he was highly criticized for making selections based on loyalty and cronyism over capability and experience. During Trump's term, there was a high turn-over of White House personnel, leaving the new team unprepared for the pandemic crisis.

(3) [**Thoughtless Inactions, Misleading and Incorrect Statements.**] Initial pandemic warnings were made formally to the White House on 3 January 2020, and repeatedly through February, by the intelligence agencies specifically about the Coronavirus. Also on 3 January, Dr. Redfield, Director of the CDC, talked by phone to his counterpart in China who warned him of a mysterious respiratory illness. This information was relayed to Dr. Alex Azar, the Secretary of Department of Health and Human Services (HHS), who in turn relayed the information to the White House. **On 21 January, a person in the state of Washington was identified by the CDC as the first confirmed case of Coronavirus in the U.S. The President said, "We have it totally under control. It's one person coming in from China, and we have it under control."**

On 28 January at President Trump's classified daily briefing, as reported by Bob Woodward in his book entitled, *"RAGE"* (Simon & Schuster), the national security advisor Robert O'Brien said to Trump, "This (the coronavirus) will be the biggest national security threat you face in your presidency. This is going to be the roughest thing you face."

On 29 January Peter Navarro, Assistant to the President, warned in an internal memorandum that "the coronavirus could evolve into a full-blown pandemic, imperiling the lives of millions of Americans".

Outside of the U.S. government, Ms. Sharon Sanders published information from her home in Winter Haven, Florida, on her blog "FluTrackers". She had been tracking information from officials in China's Hubei province who had announced on 31 December 2019 an outbreak of an unusual cluster of pneumonia cases. She also said there were a number of cases in hospitals in Wuhan, China, but the cause was not clear. On 6 January 2020, the New York Times noted "pneumonia-like illness sickened 59 people in Wuhan". Two days later, The Washington Post and AP staff published short stories. On 20 January, mainstream Fox News asked a question on the topic in an interview.

(4) [**Demeaning and Blaming Others, Without Merit.**] On 5 January 2020, the World Health Organization (WHO) posted a Defense Outbreak News report on the 31 December 2019 "pneumonia clusters" in China and reported as of 3 January, a total of 44 patients with pneumonia of unknown cause have been reported to WHO by international authorities. **Later, in April 2020, President Trump complained about WHO not providing early coronavirus information to the United States, but this was not the case.**

(5) [**Lack of Understanding, Too Little and Too Late Action.**] On

30 January, the WHO declared a Global Health Emergency and the U.S. State Department warned travelers to avoid China. On 31 January, the White House put a ban on airline travel from China and on 11 March from Europe as an effort to stop the Coronavirus from spreading widely into the United States. **Unfortunately, despite President Trump's claim that "We got it early," it was reported that 300,000 people came into the U.S. from China during the cornavirus period before the ban and 40,000 came in after the ban. In addition, many people came into the U.S. "through the back door," as noted by New York Governor Andrew Cuomo, from Europe before the European ban was declared, leading to the coronavirus catastrophe in New York City. These two delayed actions by the White House, especially the delayed travel ban for Europe, made the crisis, much, much worse.**

Meanwhile, by the end of January the global number of coronavirus cases grew to 9,800 cases and 213 deaths.

(B) TRUMP FAILURES LEADING TO THE FIRST CORONAVIRUS "EXPLOSION"

(6) [**Lack of Preparation and Testing Capability**.] On 6 February, a person died from the coronavirus in California. However, this information was not known to the California or White House authorities or the news media at the time due to a lack of coronavirus testing capability. The coroner was suspicious of the patient's symptoms and sent a sample of her tissue to the CDC. The CDC later determined that the cause of death was indeed the coronavirus. This result indicates that the coronavirus was already in California before Trump declared the first travel ban. A

second death occurred in California on 17 February. Previously, the first coronavirus death was thought to be on 29 February. If the CDC testing capability was available on 6 February, the CDC would most likely have known about the first coronavirus death three weeks earlier than the events that occurred in real time. This could have had an important impact on the start date of coronavirus social distancing mitigation methods.

(7) [**Lack of Understanding and Inept, misleading and wishful Statements.**] **On 7 February, Bob Woodward tape recorded an interview phone call from President Trump. While discussing the coronavirus, the president said, "It goes through the air. It's also more DEADLY than even your strenuous flus." President Trump knew the coronavirus was "DEADLY".** During February, President Trump continued to down play Coronavirus Crisis and to mislead the public by making totally inept, misleading, and wishful statements, such as "The virus is a hoax."; "We'll have a vaccine in a month."; "One day, it's like a miracle, It will disappear." In downplaying the coronvirus by indicating it was not DEADY, President Trump was misleading the American people.

(8) [**Inability to Know Right from Wrong, Thoughtless action and Incorrect Statement.**] On 25 February Dr. Nancy Messonnier, Director for the National Center for Immunization and Respiratory Diseases (NCIRD), said, "The CDC was preparing for a pandemic. It's not a question of if this will happen but when this will happen and how many people in this country will have severe illnesses." It was reported the next day that President Trump was angry with Dr. Messonnier for her true statement and she was reprimanded.

Clearly, President Trump did not know right from wrong (a) when he reprimanded Dr. Messonnier and (b) when he said the next day that the number of the coronavirus cases would go to about zero in a couple of days. At this point, the stock market was showing volatility.

(9) [**Incredible Lack of Understanding and Inept, Incorrect Statement.**] **On 26 February, President Trump said "When you have 15 [cases in the United States], and the 15 within a couple of days is going to be down to close to zero, that's a pretty good job we've done."**

February 26 is an important date since with just 15 known cases the CDC was trying to contact trace the Corona virus cases; however, the contact tracing failed because there were so many unknown cases in the U.S.

One month later, on 26 March, the U.S. will lead the world in the number of confirmed coronavirus cases with 81,321 and more than 1000 deaths.

(10) [**Lack of Understanding of the Problem.**] During the month of February, the United States shipped millions of dollars worth of medical equipment, including face masks, ventilators and protective garments, to China, with federal endorsement. This demonstrates the total lack of understanding by the White House of the potential coronavirus threat.

On 1 March, the first coronavirus case was confirmed in New York City. On 7 March, Gov. Cuomo issued a state of emergency order for New York State.

(11) [**Lack of Concern for People**.] On 6 March, the incident of U.S. coronavirus patients on the Grand Princess cruise ship off the coast of San Francisco offers insight in President Trump's self interest and lack of concern for others. When asked about his recommendations for the ship and its sick passengers, Trump responded, **"If it were up to me I would leave them out there. Why should we bring them back in here and raise the numbers?"**

(12) [**Thoughtless Inaction**.] On 9 March, after one of the worst weeks in stock market trading since 2007-08, all three Wall Street indices fell 7%. During January and February President Trump did very little to deal with the coronavirus. However, after the drops in the Wall Street market indices, the coronavirus finally got President Trump's serious attention as a major concern for the United States. The business community saw the problem before Trump did.

On 10 March, Dr, Fauci, Director of The National Institute of Allergy and Infectious Diseases (NIAID) of the National Institute of Health (NIH), said that "the novel coronavirus is 10 times more lethal than the seasonal flu." At a House hearing, where he warned that the U.S. must take serious mitigation efforts now. **"Bottomline: It's going to get worse if we don't take serious mitigation now. What's going to happen is we're going to be weeks behind." At this point, the federal government was already months behind, but the White House did not realize it.**

The coronavirus at this point was considered very dangerous, 10 times more lethal than the seasonal flu. About 36,000 people died from the flu in the 2017-18 season. This indicates that over 360,000 people could die in the U.S. this year from the coronavirus, since it is also more contagious than the flu. About 50% of the people who contracted the virus were asymptomatic and spread the disease without knowing it. In addition, the disease appeared to be contagious in the first 2 to 3 days before symptoms were detected.

(13) [**Lack of Understanding, Too Late and Too Little Action.**] On 11 March, the White House declared a travel ban on travel from Europe. This action was way too late. The crisis was already in New York State. Governor Cuomo previously declared a state of emergency on 7 March with 89 people confirmed to be sick with the coronavirus.

(14) [**Inaccurate Statements, Lack of Understanding.**] On 13 March, President Trump states that the coronavirus "came out of nowhere" and "This blindsided the world and I think we handled it very well." These statements are inaccurate. The coronavirus came out of China and on 3 January, a notice of the virus was relayed by phone to Dr. Redfield, Director of the CDC, from his counterpart in China. The White House was warned soon after Dr. Redfield's phone call to China. The portion of the statement indicating "that we handled it very well" is grossly inaccurate and misleading.

(15) [**Inability to Plan, Too Little and Too Late Action; Demeaning and blaming others without merit (including the truthful news media and the U.S. intelligence community);**] On 13 March, after the problems on Wall Street and Dr. Fauci's warning that "it's going to get worse," President Trump declared a National Health Emergency. Note, this action was only 16 days after Trump declared that the number of coronavirus cases would go

down close to zero in a couple of days. Again, this action was too late and too little since the medical equipment and facilities were not in place to deal with the crisis that was happening at that moment.

Also on 13 March, President Trump declared "I don't take responsibility at all" and blames "set of circumstances, rules, regulations and specifications from a different time", when questioned about the administrations delays in coronavirus testing.

On 16 March, Dr. Sara Cody and a courageous group of public health officers of Santa Clara County issued a stay-in-place order for the San Francisco Bay Area. Three days later on 19 March, Gov. Newsom of California issued a state-wide stay-at-home order for the entire state after warning that 56% of the state is at risk; the stay-at-home order required everyone to stay home except for essentials like buying groceries or seeking medical care. On the next day, New York State issued a similar order. Additional mitigation techniques, such as social distancing, were also put in place.

(16) [**Misleading Statement.**] On 26 March, the CDC released a report on the first 508 people hospitalized in the U.S. with the coronavirus. Of these, 38% were between 20 and 54 years old. Half of those ending up in intensive care were younger than 50. Early in the year, President Trump told the public that the virus does not appear to affect younger people. This dangerously suggested that younger people did not need to worry about the virus. As a result, younger people were spreading the disease in Florida and New Orleans on spring breaks and at "coronavirus

parties". Unfortunately, many younger people were contracting and spreading the disease because many were asymptomatic and did not know they were doing this.

(17) [**Too Little and Too Late Action**.] On 27, 28 and 20 March, respectively, President Trump signed a $2 Trillion stimulus bill, the CDC urged residents of New York, New Jersey and Connecticut to refrain from nonessential domestic travel for 14 days, and Virginia, Maryland and the District of Columbia issued orders requiring residents to stay home.

 (18) [**Incredible Lack of Understanding and Ego-driven, Self-Promotion**.] **By 26 March, one month after Trump stated that the number of cases would go to about zero in a couple of days, there were a total of 81,321 cases and 1000 deaths due to the coronavirus in the U.S. The medical worker heroes and the first responder heroes were dying. People were dying alone in the hospitals without family members present. New York City hospitals were being overrun with cases. Hospital personnel were overrun with sick patients and dying because of a lack of medical protection equipment. The dead were put into awaiting refrigerated tracker trailer trucks. Meanwhile, on television nearly each day at the Presidential Task Force meetings, President Trump responded with continual bragging and false statements about the White House exaggerated accomplishments, as these good people are sick and dying.**

By 2 April, the global number of coronavirus cases grew to 1 million in over 171 countries, 10 million Americans are out of work and 6.6 Million applied for unemployment.

(19) [**Refusal to Deal in the Truth.**] On 3 April, The Washington Post documented more than 18,000 false or misleading statements by President Trump since becoming president.

(20) [**Too Little and Too Late**.] On 3 April, the CDC urged all Americans to wear a mask if they expect to be outdoors in an area where they cannot maintain a safe 6 foot distance from other people. However, President Trump said he was not going to wear a mask, somewhat undermining the CDC guidelines and safety measures. **As it will later turn out, this lack of support for the CDC by President Trump was another big mistake.**

(21) [**Lack of Understanding**.] On 10 April, President Trump said, "When somebody's President of the United States the authority is total." Trump used his daily press conference to say that he would soon tell the country when he planned to open the country up. He said, "I'm going to have to make a decision. I would say without question, it's the biggest decision I've ever had to make." It turns out that Trump does not have the legal authority to make this decision; it lies with the governors of each state.

(22) [**Inability to Know Right From Wrong, Lack of Ethical Standards.**] On 20 April, Dr. Rick Bright, former director of the Biomedical Advanced Research and Development Authority (BARDA), was reassigned. On 5 May, Dr. Bright alleged in a whistleblower complaint that he was reassigned because he tried to "prioritize science and safety over political expediency". Dr. Bright asserted that he resisted government leadership to make "potentially harmful drugs widely available," including chloroquine and hydroxychloroquine. President Trump had repeatedly urged people take these drugs to fight the coronavirus.

The drugs were approved for limited hospital patients with COVID-19. However, preliminary studies found COVID-19 patients treated with hydroxychloroquine could have serious side effects. The general public was taking the drug based on President Trump's recommendation: "What have you got to lose?"

Further, Dr. Bright alleges that he was trying to sound the alarm about the virus beginning in early January, calling for the rapid development of treatments and vaccines and increasing the stockpile of N95 masks and ventilators, at a time when HHS political leadership appeared to him as underestimating the threat.

On 22 April, the Food and Drug Administration (FDA) warned against the use of hydroxychloroquine, an anti-malarial drug Trump had repeatedly promoted as a cure for sick coronavirus patients, because it can cause serious heart problems and sometimes death. Also, the FDA posted a warning not to take chloroquine.

(23) [**Thoughtless Statement and Incredibly Dangerous Lack of General Knowledge.**] On 23 April at the daily Presidential Task Force Meeting, **President Trump dangerously suggested that injecting disinfectants into the body might cure patients suffering from the coronavirus.** The federal government immediately issued warnings to people not to inject, or take into their bodies in any way, the poisonous disinfectants. There was much outcry and many phone calls over the President's "Dangerous Cure".

(24) [**Stunning Lack of Understanding and Leadership.**] **On 28**

April, the coronavirus crisis in the United States hit two catastrophe-level milestones. First, the number of confirmed cases exceeded the I Million mark at 1,010,717. Globally, the U.S. has approximately one-third of the total number of global confirmed cases, which is 3,110,219. Second, the total number of U.S. deaths is 58,365; this number exceeds the total number of deaths during the Vietnam War. Globally, the U.S. has approximately one-quarter of the global deaths, which is 216,808. These reported numbers are catastrophic changes in just over two months. For, comparison, the U.S. has less than 5% of the global population.

Dr. Fauci, the well-respected Director of NIAID at NIH, commented on the unprecedented change in numbers as, "IT EXPLODED." This unprecedented " EXPLOSION " to over 1 million confirmed U.S. coronavirus cases on 28 April comes about two months after President Trump stated on 26 February when there were 15 confirmed cases that "the number of confirmed cases would go to about zero in a couple of days". This one statement demonstrates the total "Lack of Understanding" President Trump had at that time or an intentional desire to Mislead the Public with a false comfort. The virus was spreading quickly, but the extent of the spread was not known due to the serious lack of testing capability.

Between 13 April and 13 June, 2020, the number of confirmed new coronavirus cases per day slowly dropped from about 30,000 to about 20,000. This was the result of the economic shutdown and the 3 April CDC recommendation for all Americans to wear a mask outside or maintain a social distance of at least 6 feet and not to meet in groups of ten or more people.

(C) TRUMP FAILURES LEADING TO THE SECOND CORONAVIRUS "EXPLOSION"

(25) [Lack of understanding; overconfidently ignoring information from experts.] At the end of May, President Trump pushed for states to on open their economies. The CDC provided three-phase opening guidelines. Each state should meet each phase guideline before the states were to open their economy to the next phase. Some states and residents opened their economies gradually; some states opened their economies completely in early June. **President Trump encouraged states to fully open their economies, which ignored the CDC guidelines to open in three phases. This was a big mistake. From about 13 June to 13 July, the number of confirmed new coronavirus cases increased from about 20,000 per day to over 60,000 per day. <u>In just one month, the number of U.S. confirmed new coronavirus cases per day increased by a factor of three</u>. On July 17, the number of confirmed U.S. coronavirus cases reached 76,384 and the number of deaths that day reached 963. Notably, the worst states were those with governors and/or citizens following President Trump philosophy of downplaying the dangers of the coronavirus.**

(26) [Inept thoughtless action; Lack of concern and respect for others; Inability to envision future consequences of his actions.] On 20 June, President Trump held a controversial campaign rally in Tulsa, OK. The rally was seen as controversial since the main purpose of the rally was to promote President Trump for re-election. And, Trump was clearly violating the CDC guidelines to not to meet in large groups of people; a majority of the attendees appeared to be not wearing a mask. Three weeks after the rally, Oklahoma officials reported record numbers of confirmed coronavirus cases per day and the seven-day average was almost six times what it was two months before in early April.

Before the rally, six of the president's pre-meeting staffers were tested and found positive for the coronavirus. After the rally, on 15 July, Oklahoma Governor Kevin Stitt, who attended President Trump's rally, became the first U.S. governor to announce he tested positive for Covid-19. On 29 June, Herman Cain, a former U.S. presidential candidate who also attended the rally, tested positive for the coronavirus and later died due to the virus on 29 July.

The Tulsa rally singularly demonstrates how President Trump let's his selfish motives and his lack of concern for others influence his decision making process. Fortunately, for the citizens, the Tulsa rally was poorly attended.

(27) [**Inability to envision future consequences of his actions; Inept, thoughtless actions; (Sometimes these actions are ego-driven and self-promotional.)**] For months, President Trump has been urged to be a role model for the public and conform to the 3 April CDC guideline to wear a mask when in public and expect to be within a six feet distance of another person. However, President Trump did not agree to do this, probably because it changed the image he wanted to project for himself as President of the United States. Unfortunately, this repeated lack of support for the CDC guideline had a negative impact on his supporters, who also did not believe they should wear a mask. Importantly,

the CDC requested people wear a mask not only to protect themselves, but, if they had contracted the coronavirus, to be less likely to transmit the virus to others in close proximity.

Senator Lamar Alexander of Tennessee said in June during a Senate hearing, "Unfortunately this simple life-saving practice has become part of a political debate that says: If you're for Trump, you don't wear a mask. If you are against Trump, you do. That is, I have suggested the president should occasionally wear a mask even thought there are not many occasions when it is necessary for him to do so. The president has millions of admirers. They would follow his lead." These millions of followers also downplayed the danger of the coronavirus just as Donald Trump downplayed the coronavirus and the guidelines of the CDC. This was one reason many states re-opened their economies too early and many people ignored the CDC guidelines and a main reason for the resurgence of the virus in June and July.

Still, it is worth noting that on 11 July, President Trump wore a mask for the first time in public during a visit to the Walter Reed National Military Medical Center. [President Trump did wear a mask previously at a Ford Motor Company plant for a very short time, but it was not in public; he said he did not want to give the news media the pleasure of taking his picture.] By 16 July, half of all states and many businesses have a mask mandate in place. In polling, a high percentage of Americans believe the CDC guidelines for wearing a mask should be followed.

(28) [**Inability to plan and organize future actions; Lack of concern and respect for others.**] On 7 July, President Trump pushed state and local authorities to re-open the schools, even as

the coronavirus is expanding at a dangerous rate. The White House and CDC were still not in agreement for a guidelines plan for the re-opening. After pushback by many communities not feeling safe enough to reopen, President Trump agreed that some schools could delay reopening and may need to incorporate remote learning. On 25 July, the CDC was finally allowed to publish the school reopening guidelines.

Two earlier studies indicate concerns for opening schools and the potential of transmitting the COVID-19 not only to the students and teachers, but to their families: (1) A February 2020 WHO report noted that "in China, human-to-human transmission of the COVID-19 is largely occurring in families." Among initial clusters studied in provinces, "most clusters (78% - 85%) have occurred in families". (2) A recent study in South Korea and reported by the CDC, of 5706 infected people and their 59,073 contacts, found children under 10 transmitted less often (5.3%) than adults while those between 10 and 19 spread the virus as well (18.6%) as adults.

President Trump is continuing to mislead the country by stating the "Children are almost immune to the virus" and "the virus does not seem to bother young people". These statements send the wrong message; young people and children tend to believe they do not be need to worry about the disease. The above studies show, and CDC reports show, that children and young adults do contract the disease, and potentially with serious effects, and they transmit the disease to other people. A main concern for school openings is the transmission of the disease to in-school teachers either from the students, other faculty or parents. Further, Dr. Leana Wen of George Washington University reports that about one-quarter of the teachers are susceptible to serious illness by contracting the disease.

(29) [**Inept, incorrect statements, false and misleading statements; (Many of President Trump's misleading statements are said with an ego-driven, self-promotional or bragging motivation.)**] On 9 July, The Washington Post reported that President Trump exceeded 20,000 false or misleading statements, demonstrating that he has continued misleading the nation well into the coronavirus pandemic.

(30) [**Inability to plan and organize future actions; Refusal to deal in the truth or reality; Thoughtless Inaction.**] By 17 July, due to President Trump's refusal to take an aggressive leadership role against the coronavirus pandemic and citizens following Trump's role model of downplaying the coronavirus, the nation finds itself in a second coronavirus "EXPLOSION". A number of Sun Belt states, including Texas, Florida, Georgia and Arizona are in a disaster/catastrophe mode with record rises in the number of cases and severe shortages of medical personnel, equipment and testing. In Texas and Arizona, the return of the refrigerated tractor trailer trucks and portable refrigerated storage coolers to the hospital morgues to store dead bodies brings back images of the New York City catastrophe.

(31) [**Lack of understanding, over-confidently ignoring information from experts; (The experts include the U.S. intelligence community, the CDC and his cabinet.); Refusal to deal in the truth; (President Trump was not honest with himself or the American public.); Thoughtless Inactions. (The resulting**

delays in acting against coronavirus pandemic were a major factor in the number of deaths recorded.)] On 21 July, after continuing to down play the dangers of the coronavirus, after a resurgence of the number of confirmed coronavirus cases rose from about 20,000 in June (stunningly about a month ago) to a record numbers of over 65,000 per day, after many hospitals in the southern states reached past their critical care limits, and after President Trump's poll ratings were taking a nose dive, President Trump finally agreed to support and endorse some the long-standing CDC statements and guidelines. Still, on the very next day after endorsing the CDC mask wearing guideline, President Trump said less enthusiastically at his next coronavirus meeting, "If you want to wear a mask, wear one." This is an indication that Donald Trump is not steadfast in his leadership.

First, Trump said about the coronavirus, "it's going to get worse before it gets better" (which is a repeat of Dr. Fauci's statement) and "that's something I don't like saying about things, but that's how it is. That's what we have." This is an about face to his earlier statements, which indicated that "We are doing a great job." and "The virus will go away soon". However, later in July, President Trump again started down playing the advantages of a mask and was not practicing the CDC recommended guidelines.

Second, President said, "We are urging state and local officials to mandate wearing a mask when social distancing is not possible." He also said, "Whether you like the mask or not, they have an impact, they'll have an effect, and we need everything we can get." The CDC announced the mask-wearing guideline on 3

April and President Trump waited 109 days to endorse the guideline. **President Trump's delay in endorsing the CDC guideline of wearing masks came after over 3.5 million additional people became sick and over one-hundred-thousand additional people died from the coronavirus.**

(32) [**Inability to work with others, intellectually, socially, ethically and legally; Refusal to deal in the truth.**] Looking back over the months of January through July 2020, President Trump has demonstrated many leadership flaws that have led to his many leadership failures. However, his inability to work hand-in-hand with the CDC and his refusal to deal in the truth that the CDC was trying to promote, were two primary leadership flaws that led to the severity of the coronavirus disaster for the citizens of the United States. If President Trump had kept the Pandemic Directorate at the White House, who worked well with the CDC, in place and then let these organizations run the show, certainly, we would be in a different place today. **It has been frustrating to see so many people get sick and so many people die simply because President Trump did not have the leadership skills, himself, to take on such an undertaking. And, he does not realize he is lacking in so many ways.**

(33) [**Refusal to deal in the truth; (President Trump was not honest with himself or the American public.)**] **On 23 July, the number of confirmed coronavirus cases cross a new milestone of over 4 million. President Trump said the reason there are so many cases is that we are testing more people. This statement is meant to divert the momentous meaning of the event from the actual reason there are so many cases: there are at least**

4,005,414 people in the U.S. who have become sick from the coronavirus. By the end of July, over 150,000 people have died due to the coronavirus.

The seriousness of this milestone and the U.S. situation can be seen by recording the number of days between each million count milestone: 99 days to reach 1 million; then 44 days to reach 2 million; then 27 days reach 3 million and then most worrisome, only 16 days to reach 4 million (and again only 16 days to reach 5 million on 8 August and still growing at a rapid pace). This is the second coronavirus "EXPLOSION". And, it is a demonstration of exponential growth (doubling every 44 days): 1 million to 2 million cases in 44 days and 2 million to 4 million cases in 43 days. If President Trump and his administration have a pandemic strategy, it is not working.

(34) [**Inability to plan and organize future actions.**] On 29 July 2020, the Association of American Medical Colleges (AAMC) published a report that warned of a potential extremely high (multiple hundreds of thousands) death toll. The report provided immediate actions that should be taken by the United States against the coronavirus pandemic:

1. Remedy critical supply shortages of supply and drug shortages.

2. Swiftly and dramatically increase availability and accessibility of testing.

3. Establish national standards on face coverings.

4. Establish and enforce national criteria for local stay-at-

home orders and reopening protocols.

5. Establish national criteria for school K – 12 re-openings and convene a working group to study different approaches.

6. Immediately expand health insurance through COBRA.

7. Beginning planning now to prioritize distribution of the SARS – COV -2 vaccines.

8. Address and resolve health care inequalities.

9. Inform. Educate and engage the public.

These proposed immediate actions are presented here to provide an indication of the actions President Trump and his administration should have taken well before this date. The lack of a documented plan and other not-taken-actions were discussed at a Congressional Hearing on 31 July.

By 8 August, the number of deaths due to the coronavirus is over 1,000 per day and the total number of confirmed cases is now over 5 million. The number of confirmed cases grew by approximately 2 million in the last month, averaging 62,500 new cases per day. And, The Washington Post reports that President Trump and his administration continue their efforts to intentionally muffle individual CDC scientists from stating their view of the pandemic status. Also, President Trump and his administration continue to downplay the CDC recommendations for virus control. This lack of a will to do everything that can be done allows the coronavirus to spread at a dangerous rate. At the same time, President Trump and his administration continue to mislead the public by painting a rosy picture of how "great" the administration is doing. After seven months of the coronavirus pandemic, the U.S. continues to be the worst performing country in the world for the number of confirmed cases, the financial losses and the number of deaths; this should not have happened.

4 UNDERSTANDING THE CORONAVIRUS "EXPLOSIONS"

Dr. Jeffrey Shaman, an epidermiologist professor at Columbia University, has explained the coronavirus "explosion" very well using a mathematical model of the virus spread. He explains that that the virus starts out with a small number of people, but swells up on you, like a tsunami wave, and overwhelms you. The virus increases in number exponentially by doubling in growth. The exponential doubling in growth is explained this way. Imagine an invasive lily plant that doubles in growth every day in a pond. Early on, there are just a small number of lilies in the pond. However, on day 30, the pond is full of lilies. Dr. Shaman then asks the question, "When was the pond half full of lilies?" The answer: it was half full on day 29, the day before. It is a strange and horrifying process.

Dr. Shaman, and his group at Columbia University, modeled the exponential growth of the coronavirus using actual data from every county in the United States over the period of 15 March to 3 May. They were keeping track of the transmissibility of the virus, which includes the effects of social distance methods, and the number of deaths due to the virus in each county. The model accurately portrayed the spread of the virus and the number of deaths in the U.S. over the test period. As a result, the researchers were confident of their model.

Then, the group did something extraordinary. They kept everything in the model the same, except they moved the implementation of the social distancing earlier by one week. The results were stunning. As reported in The Washington Post on 21 May, the model showed that the total number of actual deaths recorded at the end of the test period on 3 May, which was 65,307, would have reduced to an estimated 29,410 deaths, if the social distancing that did occur, happened one week earlier. That is, the number of deaths would be an estimated 55% less, if the social distancing had been adopted just one week earlier. [And, the number of deaths would be an estimated 83% less, the vast majority, if President Trump acted just two weeks earlier.] This remarkable result links an estimated number of deaths to President Trump's thoughtless delay in taking action for social distancing, or in taking any mitigation action. Dr. Shaman also explains that we cannot be complacent and need to keep the number of cases small while we hold on and try to come up with a vaccine or effective therapeutics. Dr. Shaman further blamed the Trump Administration for failing to develop a powerful national system for testing, tracing and isolating sickened people.

Dr. David Ho, also of Columbia University, discussed on MSNBC two strategies for the United States to deal with the coronavirus. The first strategy was for all of the states to have a united strategy of fighting the coronavirus simultaneously and together. This strategy was being used with the support of the CDC and most of the American people (and to a lesser degree President Trump and his followers) in April and May of 2020. But, in early April, President Trump indicated his lack of support for the economy shutdown and suggested the economies open as early as 12 April for Easter. Fortunately, President Trump backed off from this very early economy opening, but still kept pushing that he would like to see it happening soon. At President Trump's strong suggestion and with the CDC guidelines in place, the state economies started to open around Memorial Day on 25 May, which was still too early. This shutdown was later described by Dr. Fauci as a 50% shutdown, instead of a more complete 95% shutdown used by successful countries fighting the virus.

Unfortunately, many states and their citizens ignored the CDC guidelines for a phased approach to opening the economy and for abiding by the CDC guidelines at all. This was the start of the second coronavirus "EXPLOSION". As Dr. Ho explained in his second strategy, the United States, due to different state laws and politics, each state is fighting the coronavirus somewhat independently and somewhat in a sequential manner due to the way the virus had spread. This second strategy is more difficult to control the virus and extends its life. After the Memorial Day economy openings and after an appropriate virus incubation period, the number of confirmed coronavirus cases in the U.S. started to grow on an exponential trajectory. This exponential growth was due to states and citizens who believed President Trump's suggestions to downplay the dangers of the virus and of totally ignoring the CDC guidelines. In the first 27 days after 11

June, the number of coronavrus cases grew by 1 million cases to a total of 3 million cases on 8 July and in the next 16 days the number of coronavirus cases grew by an additional 1 million and again in next 16 days it grew by 1 million cases for a total of 5 million cases on 8 August. The U.S. was indeed well into its second coronavirus "EXPLOSION".

The above "EXPLOSION" seems hard to envision, but, as reported in The Washington Post on 19 July, the situation can be explained by a simple account of the patrons in the Harper's Restaurant and Brew Pub in East Lansing, MI. The local county health officer, Ms. Linda Vail, tracked the number of coronavirus cases at the location during the 30 day period of 17 June to 17 July. The cases went from 2 on 18 June, to 88 on 28 June, to 171 on 7 July and to 187 on 17 July. If the 187 new cases occurred in 10,000 locations across the U.S., it is easy to envision how 1.87 million new cases could occur across the U.S. during this 30 day period. This is an example of the exponential growth of the coronavirus.

The above restaurant example can be frightening when considered as a similar cluster example for in-person schools, which President Trump proposed for reopening this August and September across the country. Consider each K – 12 school as a potential (multiple) cluster starter. There are over 100,000 schools in the U.S. and, if you assume just 10% of the schools have a starter infection, this leads to a potential 10,000 (or more given there could be multiple clusters per school) new cluster locations. Hopefully, this would not happen since the government could step in to prevent large cluster developments. But, this example does present the potential dangers of opening in-person schools as opposed to remote-learning schools.

President Trump's Coronavirus Disaster

5 CORONAVIRUS EVENT SUMMARY

The United States places high emphasis on medical research. Further, the country has the finest hospitals, the best medical equipment, pharmaceutical companies and medical equipment manufacturers. The coronavirus crisis effects would be much, much worst if these medical capabilities were not in place. The hospital workers and first responders worked courageously and tirelessly to help the coronavirus patients. The extraordinary efforts of the medical community, and others that helped people during the coronavirus crisis, cannot be overstated. The entire nation appreciates their help.

The coronavirus events described in the section appeared to be unlikely in the United States. However, President Trump's apparent lack of concern for U.S. citizens, his delay in taking action, downplaying of the dangers of the virus and his misleading of the country with false and misleading statements have led a very capable country into a disaster situation for the physical and emotional and financial well being of its people.

By the end of April 2020, the United States is well into its worst situation since World War II. Most states are still in lockdown. There are roughly 30 million people (14.7%) who have filed for unemployment in the last 6 weeks (to have a comparison, 8.7 million people filed for unemployment during the Great Recession of 2007-2008). Many businesses are on the verge of going out of business. The federal government has spent trillions of dollars, and is planning to spend trillions more, to assist people and businesses severely affected by the coronavirus pandemic. Local and state governments are also in a financial crisis. The current debt is at the highest level since 1945, after World War II, and there is a concern in Congress and among economists about the high level of U.S. debt. The first quarter Gross Domestic Product (GDP) has dipped 4.7%; this only includes less than one month of the severe portion of the coronavirus.

By 27 May, over 100,000 people have died from the coronavirus. This striking milestone gave pause to the country, especially occurring just after the Memorial Day weekend. According to the Columbia University study, discussed in the fourth section, the vast majority of these deaths can be attributed to the thoughtless delays by President Trump and his administration in taking a national leadership role in mitigation actions. As May comes to an end, all the U.S. states have started opening their economies, to varying degrees. However, the states are doing this with CDC mitigation guidelines in place. The President's support for the CDC guidelines has varied. The future remains somewhat uncertain, but the economy must start to get back on track. At this point, the state economies are about to start opening.

By 27 July, two months later, 138,016 people have died

from the coronavirus. This striking jump in the number of cases is due to President Trump's emphasis to open the state economies, without each state meeting the CDC benchmarks. Many state governors and citizens did not support the CDC guideline for the use of protective masks and social distancing. As a result, a number of the states went into a crisis with the lack of testing capabilities to produce quick test results, the lack of medical equipment and overwhelmed medical personnel. The second quarter GDP dropped 9.5%. This is a record setting quarterly drop; the worst drop since at least 1875. All three months of the quarter are during the coronavirus. For the first half year of 2020, the GDP dropped 15.2 %; this indicates the financial difficulty the nation is experiencing during the pandemic.

The Coronavirus in the U.S. did not have to be this bad. It is worth comparing the number of deaths in the U.S. with other countries. The U.S. has by far the highest number of coronavirus deaths. By comparison, South Korea had 269 deaths compared to the U.S. 100,000 deaths, and the U.S. has only about 7 times the South Korean population. By comparison, Europe also was doing much better than the U.S. When comparing the U.S. coronavirus response to that of Europe, Dr. Fauci explained that Europe had a 95% economy shutdown while the U.S. had a 50% shutdown; he also added that the U.S. started reopening the economy too early, when there were still about 20,000 new cases per day. The number of new cases per day should have been much lower before opening the economy. The South Korea and Europe [and Canada and China] comparisons demonstrate the striking lack of leadership by President Trump and his administration in taking mitigation actions to reduce the number of deaths due to the coronavirus.

At the end of July 2020, the United States is not in a good medical place with covid-19. Dr. David Skorton, President of the AAMC, reported on 29 July that **"Cases continue to rise at an alarming rate across much of the United States. If the nation does not change its course – and soon – deaths in the U.S. could well be in the multiples of hundreds of thousands."**

6 CONCLUSION AND FINAL THOUGHTS

President Trump's leadership failures escalated the coronavirus to be <u>both</u> the worst health disaster in the last 100 years <u>and</u> the worst financial disaster since 1932, the Great Depression. This letter provides the facts and the analyses of President Trump's innate leadership flaws and his demonstrated leadership failures that lead to the conclusion that President Trump is surely the worst U.S. President in the last 80 years, possibly ever.

President Trump's disregard for the health and well being of the American people has continued throughout the crisis. Yet, President Trump continued to say "We did a great job!" with the virus. President Trump's leadership failures include the following:

(1) He dismantled of the pandemic capability at the White House in 2018;

(2) Knowing the coronavirus was DEADLY, he intentionally deceived the American public in February by declaring " It's a hoax!" and (just 16 days before declaring the

pandemic a national emergency) " The number of cases will go close to zero in a couple of days.";

(3) He allowed of the coronavirus pandemic to travel "in the back door" from Europe to New York City, which started the first coronavirus "EXPLOSION" reaching over 1 million total confirmed cases;

(4) His thoughtless delays during late January, February and early March 2020 in taking meaningful actions resulted in the spread of the virus across the U.S. and a majority of the coronavirus deaths. (Dr. Shaman of Columbia University estimated 83% of the deaths due to a two-week delay and the spread);

(5) Knowing the coronavirus was DEADLY, he refused to listen to warnings and pleas from CDC and medical experts as he downplayed the dangers of the virus during the economic shutdown. (Dr. Fauci estimated the shutdown to be a 50% economic shutdown; a 95% shutdown was achieved in successful countries);

(6) He pressured the state governors and citizens to reopen their economies too early starting the end of May, when the virus was still dangerous and experiencing about 20,000 new coronavirus cases per day;

(7) He ignored the CDC guidelines for three-phased opening of the state economies and continuing to downplay the dangers of the virus, the wearing of a mask and social distancing, which led to the second coronavirus "EXPLOSION" reaching a total of over 6.8 million total confirmed cases and surpassing

200,000 deaths (a 19 September 2020 update).

All of these leadership failures lead to the conclusion that President Trump and his administration are clearly responsible for the <u>severity</u> of the coronavirus disaster in the United States. And, he continues to disregard the health and well being of the nation and to dangerously mislead the country.

President Trump's most consistently used and most irrational leadership flaws are his "Refusal to Deal in Truth" and his "False and Misleading Statements". It is remarkable that so many American citizens would allow him to be so untruthful and inaccurate for so long, especially with the coronavirus disaster happening right in front of their eyes and ears.

According to The Washington Post Fact Checker, on 9 July 2020, President Trump exceeded a total of 20,000 false or misleading statements during his term in office. Dr. Mary Trump, President Trump's niece and a clinical psychologist, when interviewed, explained this lack of integrity as being instilled and fortified by his father Fred Trump, Sr. Yet, many U.S. community leaders, who are normally people of high integrity, mistakenly placed, and continue to place, their trust in Donald Trump.

President Trump is not honest with himself. He portrays himself as a "genius" president, similar to a movie actor. A large portion of Americans were fooled by this portrayal into thinking he is a "genius" president. In doing this, they are not being honest to themselves or to others when discussing Trump. As the coronavirus has progressed, it is being made more apparent to Trump supporters, and to President Trump himself, that he is not the "genius" actor-president he pretends to be, but a person who has made serious mistakes trying to maintain this image. This is a painful experience for all Americans.

In "normal" times, President Trump's "false or misleading statements" appeared to be cast off or ignored or put-up-with. However, in pandemic times, when over 6.8 million people are sick and over 2.0 hundred-thousand have died and over 30 million people have been put out of work and the second quarter Gross Domestic Product (GDP) has dropped 9.5% (the largest drop in U.S. history), it is difficult to listen to the President of the United States continually boasting "We are doing a great job." When he does this, he is misleading the country as he speaks. The blame for these catastrophic numbers lies squarely with President Trump and his administration.

To his credit, Donald Trump has a number of leadership attributes which have contributed to his rise to the presidency, including: (1) he looks somewhat presidential; (2) he has commanding, although misleading, communications with an audience; and (3) he has an exceptional ability to sell most anything. Unfortunately, his ability to sell most anything has contributed to both his leadership successes and his leadership failures. His leadership successes have mostly been in real estate, where selling is a very important attribute. His leadership failures, based on selling, have mainly been in other venture activities, and these have been costly. Examples of these costly ventures include Trump University, Trump Airlines, Trump Casinos and the Trump presidency. The question is, "Who pays for these costly ventures?" The answer is the people who have been sold, or conned into, these ventures. For example: for Trump University the students pay; for Trump Airlines and Casinos the banks and his business associates pay; (Trump was reported to owe 300 million dollars to the over-seas Deutsch bank, which is currently under investigation for suspicious activities with Donald Trump.) and for the Trump presidency, the American people pay. It is the American people who have to pay the additional health (and funeral), financial and emotional costs, which were caused by President Trump's coronavirus leadership failures.

This writing is a call for all Americans to be honest with themselves and to each other. <u>Surely, we all can see: Our nation is based on trust and we must deal in the truth.</u> Donald Trump, during his rise to the presidency, took advantage of this American trust by using his "False and Misleading Statements" to gain the trust of many Americans. Unfortunately, he has betrayed this trust. Based on President Trump's lack of integrity, innate leadership flaws and demonstrated leadership failures during the coronavirus disaster, the concluding statement is:

"You Can't Trust Trump!"

Honest Abe

August 2020

P.S.   This comprehensive letter is for the general public as an honest report, as best the pseudonym author can do. It is the truthful message that matters, not the messenger.